EASY ANSWERS

TO FIRST SCIENCE QUESTIONS ABOUT

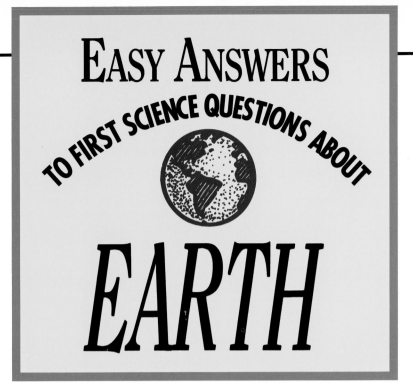

EARTH

WRITTEN BY Q. L. PEARCE

ILLUSTRATED BY GIL HUNG

EXPERT CONSULTANTS: Mycol Doyle, Ph.D., Lecturer in Botany, California Polytechnic State University, San Luis Obispo, California, and Richard Robinson, Professor of Geology, Santa Monica College, Santa Monica, California

TO GLADIE DYE

An RGA Book

ISBN 0-8317-2585-0

Q: HOW OLD IS THE EARTH?

Answer: Planet Earth is about 4.6 *billion* years old. Some 5 billion years ago, our Sun formed from a huge, spinning cloud of gas and dust in space. Circling the newborn Sun, the remains of the cloud gathered into whirling pockets of material that formed the planets. Over millions of years the young Earth first heated, then slowly cooled again and developed a hard outer crust. The oldest rocks discovered from that crust are about 3.8 billion years old.

Q: WHAT IS INSIDE PLANET EARTH?

Answer: The Earth is made up of several layers. As the planet formed, the heaviest materials (metals such as nickel and iron) sank to the center and became what is now Earth's solid core. The next layer is a liquid layer made up mostly of molten iron and nickel. Next is the thickest layer, called the mantle. It consists of rock as soft as taffy! We live on Earth's thin, hard outer layer, or crust.

crust

mantle

←outer core

←inner core

A cutaway view of the Earth

Q: HOW DO ROCKS FORM?

Answer: There are three main types of rock, and each forms in a different way. Igneous rocks are made of molten material from within the Earth that cools and becomes solid. Sedimentary rocks develop when loose materials, or sediments, such as sand or mud, are squeezed and cemented together. Metamorphic rocks are rocks that, under great heat and pressure, change into new rock that is different in form or texture from the parent rock.

Q: WHAT IS SOIL?

Answer: Soil is loose material that blankets much of the rocky surface layer of Earth's dry land. Soil supports plant life. It is made up of tiny particles of rocks and minerals as well as bits and pieces of other things, such as the rotted remains of leaves. Soil may be light and sandy or heavy, thick, and rich in clay. The type of soil that covers an area depends on many things, including the climate, vegetation, and underlying rock.

As the Earth orbits the Sun,

Earth's
axis

Sun

the seasons change

Q: *WHAT CAUSES THE SEASONS?*

Answer: The seasons are caused by the changing position of our planet in relation to the Sun. Earth is tilted on its axis (an imaginary line that runs through the planet from pole to pole). During Earth's yearly orbit, first one hemisphere and then the other tilts toward the Sun. The hemisphere tipped toward the Sun enjoys summer, and the hemisphere that is tilted away experiences winter. In between, both hemispheres experience either spring or fall.

Q: WHAT IS WIND?

Answer: Wind is moving air. Because the Earth is curved, the Sun heats our planet unevenly. Worldwide winds are caused when warm air at the equator rises, flows toward the poles, cools, becomes heavier, and descends. This cooler air from the poles then moves toward the equator to replace the warm rising air. Because of the Earth's rotation, at the equator, this circulating air flows from east to west, forming the trade winds.

Q: WHERE DOES DEW COME FROM?

Answer: Dew forms when water vapor in the air condenses, or turns into liquid water. Each day, water evaporates from oceans, lakes, and rivers and becomes a gas known as water vapor. Warm air holds a lot of water vapor. As this warm air cools during the night, it holds less and less water vapor. The point at which it can no longer hold any water vapor is called the dew point. The water then condenses in droplets on objects such as grass and spider webs.

Q: WHAT ARE CLOUDS MADE OF?

Answer: Clouds are made of tiny ice crystals or very tiny water droplets. As warm air near the ground rises, it slowly cools. Water vapor in the cooling air condenses into extremely small water droplets on airborne dust or smoke particles. If the air is cold enough, the water droplets freeze into tiny ice crystals. The droplets or ice crystals form clouds. There are three main forms of clouds: cirrus ("curl"), cumulus ("heap"), and stratus ("layer") clouds.

Q: WHAT IS THE HOTTEST PLACE ON EARTH?

Answer: The highest air temperature ever recorded was in Al'Aziziyah, Libya, where the thermometer once showed a sizzling 136 degrees Fahrenheit. Death Valley, in the southwestern United States, is not far behind. With a record high of 134 degrees, it is the hottest place in North America. The highest *average* temperature occurs at Dallol, Ethiopia. This hot spot has an overall yearly temperature of 94 degrees.

Q: WHAT IS THE COLDEST PLACE ON EARTH?

Answer: The coldest place on Earth is the continent of Antarctica. The temperature rarely rises above freezing, even in summer. A record-breaking low of −128 degrees Fahrenheit was set near Vostok Station, a Soviet research facility near the Antarctic coastline. This same area is known to have the coldest *average* temperature: a shivery −72 degrees.

Q: WHY ARE SOME MOUNTAINS ALWAYS CAPPED WITH SNOW?

Answer: Some mountains are always snowcapped because the air at the top is thin and cold. Air absorbs heat from both the Sun and the Earth. On a high mountaintop, the air is thinner and can absorb less heat. The air is thus colder, so snow doesn't melt. For every thousand feet you go up, the temperature drops by about four degrees. The snowline is the point above which snow can last all year round.

Q: DO MOUNTAINS LAST FOREVER?

Answer: No. Over millions of years, even the mightiest mountains are worn away by the action of water, ice, and wind. This destruction is called weathering and erosion. Ice can chill and crack rocks. Glaciers slide down mountainsides, carving valleys and pushing rocks and rubble ahead of them. Rain and rivers erode mountains and carry pebbles and sand to the sea. But this process is very slow: mountains erode as little as 3½ inches every 1,000 years!

Q: WHY DO RIVERS CURVE?

Answer: Curves result from changes in a river's flow. A swirl of water near one side (or bank) of a river can create a slight curve in the flow. On the outside of the curve, the rapidly flowing water cuts into the riverbank, and carries away particles of sand or mud. On the inside of the curve, the water flows more slowly and so deposits the particles of sand and mud. As one bank is worn away, the opposite bank builds up, creating a curve in the river.

Q: WHAT IS THE WORLD'S HIGHEST WATERFALL?

Answer: The world's highest waterfall is Angel Falls in Venezuela, South America. From the top of a flat plateau known as Devil's Mountain, the Rio (Spanish for "river") Caroni tumbles over a sheer cliff and splashes to a valley floor, 3,212 feet below. Angel Falls is twenty times higher than North America's Niagara Falls. It was named for James Angel, an American adventurer who discovered the remarkable waterfall in 1935.

Q: WHAT IS A SALT LAKE?

Answer: All lakes contain some minerals and salts from the surrounding land. The minerals and salts dissolve into rainwater, which then empties into the lakes. When the amount of these materials is more than three percent of the lake's contents, the lake is called a salt lake. In many cases, as water slowly evaporates from such a lake, the salts are left behind and the lake becomes even saltier. The saltiest (and largest) salt lake in North America is Utah's Great Salt Lake.

Q: *Where does oil come from?*

Answer: The oil we use probably formed from plankton (tiny plants and animals that live in the sea) and from plants that once grew in swamps. Millions of years ago, these plants and animals became buried under tons of sediment. Under heat and pressure, the material developed into gas and oil. In some places, the oil moved upward through porous rock, until its path was blocked by a layer of nonporous rock. The oil then gathered into the pools from which we pump it.

cap rock

gas

oil pocket

reservoir rock

Cross section of rock shows pools of oil and gas collected deep beneath the ground

Q: WHY ARE PLANTS GREEN?

Answer: Green plants get their color from the chlorophyll (KLOR-uh-fil) they contain. A green plant uses water and carbon dioxide from the air to make its own food. This process is called photosynthesis (fo-toe-SIN-thuh-sis). The energy needed to fuel this process comes from sunlight, and chlorophyll is needed to absorb the sunlight. The chlorophyll absorbs all the colors in sunlight except green, which it reflects. So, to us, plants appear to be green.

Q: DOES GRASS HURT WHEN IT IS CUT?

Answer: No. Grass doesn't feel anything when it is cut. Animals feel pain through certain body cells called nerve cells. Plants do not have nerve cells and so do not feel pain. For the same reason, it doesn't hurt you to have your hair or fingernails cut, since there are no nerve cells in hair or fingernails.

Q: DO PLANTS BREATHE?

Answer: Plants do not "breathe" in the same way that people do. However, they do take in and release certain gases from the atmosphere. Plants take in air through tiny openings in their leaves called stomata (a single opening is called a stoma). They use the carbon dioxide that is in the air in their food-making process (photosynthesis). The plants then release oxygen into the atmosphere through their stomata. Almost all of the oxygen in our atmosphere comes from photosynthesis.

stoma

Microscopic view of a leaf

Q: WHY DO SOME FLOWERS SMELL GOOD?

Answer: The flowers of some plants are sweet-scented and colorful to help the plants attract insects (or sometimes birds or bats) to the nectar the insects like to eat. The insects then help the plants to reproduce. When it is gathering nectar, an insect may become dusted with the pollen that's inside the flower. After dining on nectar, the insect then carries the pollen to the next flower that attracts its attention. By carrying pollen from one flower to another, insects help plants to reproduce.

Q: WHAT IS A SEED?

Answer: A seed is a reproductive body of a flowering (fruit producing) or cone-bearing plant. Seeds are produced when male and female plant cells combine in the flower or cone. Each seed is covered by a tough, waterproof outer coat, and it contains enough food for a new plant to grow. Seeds may be carried far from the parent plant by wind, water, or animals.

Cross section of an apple, showing seeds

Q: DO ALL PLANTS HAVE SEEDS?

Answer: No. Nonflowering plants, such as ferns, reproduce by means of spores that develop under their leaves. Spores that are released and land in moist ground may grow into tiny gametophytes (guh-MEET-uh-fyts), which are an early stage in the formation of a new plant. Male and female cells from the gametophytes then join to produce the new plant.

Q: WHY DO PLANTS NEED WATER?

Answer: Plants need water for their food-making process (photosynthesis). Water also helps to keep the plants' cells rigid. Without water, a plant soon droops and withers. Since plants lose a lot of water through their leaves (in the form of water vapor), the water must be replaced. So, most plants soak up water from the soil through their roots. Systems of tiny tubes in the plants' stems then carry the water to the leaves.

Q: WHY DO SOME TREES LOSE THEIR LEAVES IN AUTUMN?

Answer: Some trees lose their leaves in autumn to conserve water, since water vapor can escape through the tiny openings (stomata) in the leaves. In winter, tree roots can't draw enough water from the frozen ground to replace the water that is lost. Thus, some trees—called deciduous (dih-SIJ-uh-wus) trees—shed their leaves so available water isn't lost through the stomata.

The root system of a tree

Q: WHY DO TREE ROOTS GROW DOWN AND BRANCHES GROW UP?

Answer: Tree roots grow in the direction of the pull of gravity. This process is called geotropism (jee-oh-TRO-piz-em). Growing down into the ground, roots anchor the plant and also gather water and nutrients from the soil. The leaves of trees are attracted to light, which is needed for photosynthesis, so the leaves and branches grow toward light. This process is called phototropism (fo-toe-TRO-piz-em).

Q: HOW LONG DO TREES LIVE?

Answer: Some bristlecone pines of North America have lived for nearly 5,000 years. Many other varieties of trees may reach several hundred years of age. However, things such as disease, insects, and changes in climate can shorten a tree's life. When a tree is cut down, there is an easy way to figure out how old it was. As a tree grows, it adds an outer layer, or growth ring, each year. By counting these rings you can tell the age of the tree.

Q: *WHAT ARE WETLANDS?*

Answer: Wetlands are areas that are a combination of land and shallow water, such as swamps, marshes, bogs, estuaries, and mud flats. Some wetlands, including swamps and marshes, may be flooded throughout the year. Some other areas of land become wetlands only during rainy seasons. Wetlands provide food and shelter for hundreds of varieties of animals, including countless birds.

Q: WHAT IS THE DIFFERENCE BETWEEN A SWAMP, A MARSH, AND A BOG?

Answer: One of the main differences between swamps, marshes, and bogs is the type of plant life found in each of these wetlands. Swamps are dominated by trees such as the cypress or mangrove. Grasses and rushes are among the most common plants growing in marshes. Bogs are covered mostly by mosses and such plants as heather and cranberries.

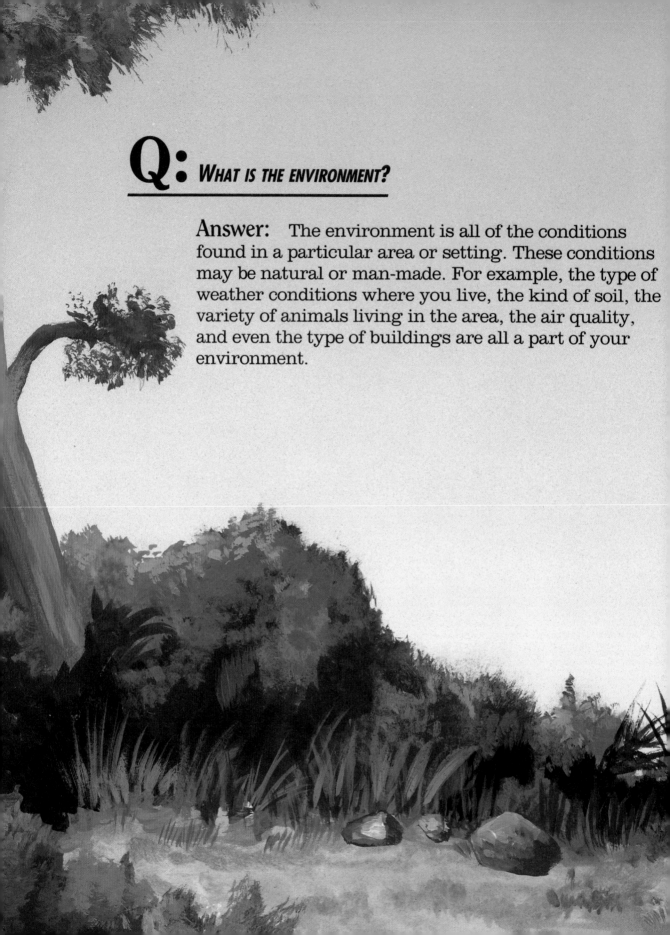

Q: *What is the environment?*

Answer: The environment is all of the conditions found in a particular area or setting. These conditions may be natural or man-made. For example, the type of weather conditions where you live, the kind of soil, the variety of animals living in the area, the air quality, and even the type of buildings are all a part of your environment.

Q: WHAT IS ECOLOGY?

Answer: Ecology is a science. It is the study of the relationship of living things to their environment and to each other. Ecologists have discovered that there is a delicate balance in nature, and that living things depend on each other to survive. It is important that we humans do our best to protect, rather than interfere with, that balance in nature. We can do this by carefully studying an area before we make changes to it.

Here are several other questions to consider about the Earth.

HAVE THE CONTINENTS ALWAYS BEEN WHERE THEY ARE TODAY?
WHAT ARE GLACIERS?
WHAT IS AN ICE AGE?
HOW DOES A CAVE FORM?
WHAT MAKES A VOLCANO EXPLODE?
WHAT CAUSES AN EARTHQUAKE?
WHAT'S THE DIFFERENCE BETWEEN A HURRICANE, A TYPHOON, AND A CYCLONE?
WHAT IS A TORNADO?
HOW OFTEN DOES LIGHTNING STRIKE THE EARTH?
HOW DOES A DESERT FORM?
WHERE ARE THE RAIN FORESTS OF THE WORLD?
CAN PEOPLE LIVE AT THE NORTH POLE?

These books will help you discover the answers:

Bresler, Lynn: *Earth Facts,* Tulsa, Oklahoma, EDC Publishing, 1986.

Gallant, Roy A.: *The Ice Ages,* New York City, Franklin Watts, 1985.

Knight, David: *The First Book of Deserts,* New York City, Franklin Watts, 1964.

Seddon, Tony, and Baily, Jill: *The Living World,* Garden City, New York, Doubleday & Co., 1986.